Tie Your Socks and Clap Your Feet

mixed-up poems by **LENNY HORT**

illustrated by **STEPHEN KRONINGER**

AN ANNE SCHWARTZ BOOK • ATHENEUM BOOKS FOR YOUNG READERS

For Sophie, the daughter I've loved since I was born.
I couldn't have eaten this book without you.
—L. H.

For, in order of appearance, Vanessa, Charlotte,
Kati, and Sophie.
—S. K.

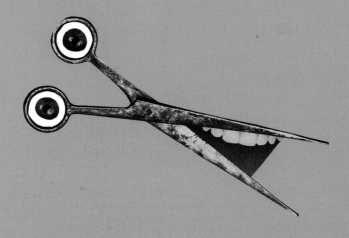

The art for this book consists of collage created from
magazine photographs and cut paper.

Atheneum Books for Young Readers
An imprint of Simon & Schuster Children's Publishing Division
1230 Avenue of the Americas
New York, New York 10020
Text copyright © 2000 by Lenny Hort
Illustrations copyright © 2000 by Stephen Kroninger
All rights reserved, including the right of reproduction in
whole or in part in any form.
Book design by Angela Carlino
The text of this book is set in Imperfect Bold
Printed in Hong Kong
10 9 8 7 6 5 4 3 2 1

Library of Congress Cataloging-in-Publication Data
Hort, Lenny.
Tie your socks and clap your feet; mixed-up poems / by
Lenny Hort; illustrated by Stephen Kroninger.—1st ed.
p. cm.   "An Anne Schwartz book."
Summary: A collection of nonsensical poems about dogs
that purr, eating soup with a knife, a baby girl with a
mustache, and other silly situations.
ISBN 0-689-83195-1
1. Children's poetry, American. [1. Humorous poetry.
2. American poetry.] I. Kroninger, Stephen, ill.
PS3558.06977T54   2000   811.54—dc21   99-27023

❋ Contents ❋

Our New House

Come and visit our new house.
I built it when I was born.
Walk out back to our front door
so you can ring the horn.

Come upstairs to the basement.
It's where we park our Jeeps
and where we keep the bathtub
where everybody sleeps.

Come downstairs to the attic,
where we eat all our books.
You'll find the shiny toilet seat
where Junior always cooks.

With doors on every ceiling
and floors to give us light,
we'll live in our new house forever.
It burned down last Saturday night.

Sweet Little Baby

Sweet little baby's just seven feet tall.
Baby, don't eat Mommy's nice bowling ball.
Baby's cute mustache is starting to curl.
What an adorable, sweet baby girl.

In Ninety Years When I Am Young

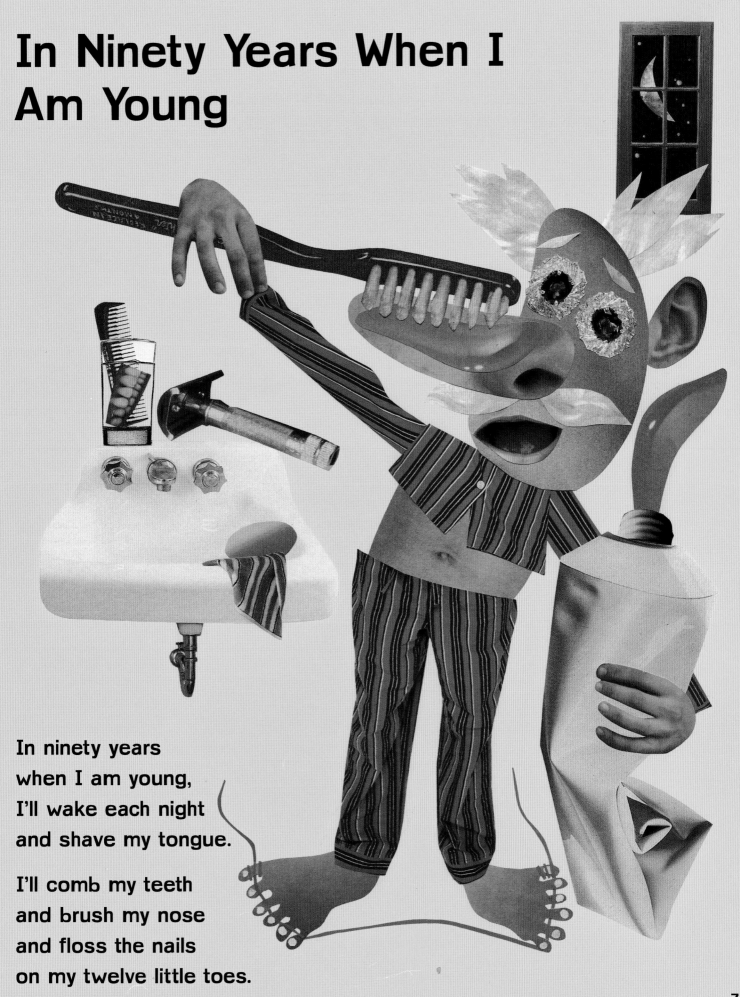

In ninety years
when I am young,
I'll wake each night
and shave my tongue.

I'll comb my teeth
and brush my nose
and floss the nails
on my twelve little toes.

A Fat Little Tomcat

A fat little tomcat
flew up a tree
to find fish feathers
to serve with tea.

He grabbed a mighty weakfish
by the thumb of its leg.
Then the fat little tomcat
laid a square little egg.

Five Hats

Grandbrother always wears five hats,
'cause five's an even letter.
He likes to swim with five pet bats,
and three are even better.

Down in the Desert

Down in the desert,
where the days are green and wet,
an Inuit dentist
kept a clam for a pet.

The clam sang as sweetly
as a grizzly bear
while helping the dentist
to cut turtles' hair.

A Pair of Purple Oranges

A pair of purple oranges—
oooh, what a treat!
Peppery cool
and lemony sweet.

A pair of yellow blueberries
fell from a tree.
I opened my nose
and drank up all three.

Time to Set the Table

Time to set the table.
What do we need?
Napkins to sit on
and dishes to read.

Knives for the soup
and spoons for the steak.
Forks for the juice
and straws for the cake.

Cups for the beans
and bowls for the bread
and chopsticks for Dad
to butter his head.

The Maestro

The maestro waves her violin.
A piano's tucked beneath her chin.
The concert's ready to begin.

The trumpet sounds its emerald strings.
The tenor shuts her mouth and sings.
The maestro's tuba rings and rings.

The harpist blows a piercing tone.
The drummer beats his saxophone.
The maestro strokes her slide trombone.

The guitar spoons its tasty tweet.
A curtain falls on every seat.
The maestro bows and claps her feet.

When the Groundhog Slides Down the Chimney

When the groundhog slides down the chimney
with his valentines up his sleeve,
carve your eggs and paint your pumpkins,
for it must be Christmas Eve.

Yes, the groundhog has eight red-nosed turkeys
to swim his sled up from the north.
Columbus, it soon will be Christmas!
Tomorrow is July the Fourth.

I Drove Over Oceans

I drove over oceans
to Tokyo, Spain,
to see a green leopardess
shaking her mane.

The leopardess barked
at my three-legged plane,
so I pedaled back home
on the wings of a train.

Broccoli Pie

On a hot snowy day
in the week of July,
Farmer Jones planted
a broccoli pie.

Nine days later
on the thirty-first of June,
there was broccoli pie
growing high as the moon.

20

I Saw It on the Radio

Late last night outside Fort Knox
the emperor learned to tie his socks.
He tied all three with cuckoo clocks—
    I saw it on the radio.

Later that day in Central Park
the emperor walked his nice pet shark.
The emperor wasn't afraid of the dark—
    I saw it on the radio.

Then finally last month in South Podunk
the emperor packed a rhinoceros trunk
with quills he plucked from a colorful skunk—
    I smelled it on the radio.

Fairy Tale

The king of New York
and her nephew, the queen,
were painting their castle
with iced gasoline,
when . . .
a sleeping prince kissed
a tadpole's warm toes
and turned herself into
a snowy blue rose,
then . . .
some giants flew by
on the shoes of some ants,
and scared a fierce mermaid
right out of his pants.

Our Pets

Tabby dog got mad
and started to purr
when I petted our goldfish's
thick purple fur.

The dog bit our Manx cat
right on her left tail,
then opened the birdcage
and swallowed our whale.

The Beast

A strange beast stole my underwear—
A beast darker than a polar bear.
A beast with more claws than a killer whale.
A beast with more speed than a two-ton snail.
No python ever had such paws.
No earthworm ever had such jaws.
More spots than a tiger, more teeth than a hen—
I don't think I'll be seeing my underwear again.

Lullaby

Open your eyes and go to sleep.
The ocean's high. The mountain's deep.
I'll keep you safe from howling sheep,
so open your eyes and go to sleep.

Stand up tall and rest your head.
The star is green. The moons are red.
Sleep safe and sound while I eat your bed.
Just stand up tall and rest your head.

Fill your feet with happy dreams
of sweetly dancing football teams.
I'll sing you to sleep with soothing screams
to fill your feet with happy dreams.

Now close your eyes, it's time to wake.
The earth sets with a gentle quake.
Come taste your breakfast rattlesnake.
Yes, close your eyes, it's time to wake.

Barnyard Babble

Me-ow, says the cow.

Moo, moo, says the shrew.

Quack, quack, says the yak.

Cluck, cluck, says the duck.

Bow-wow, says the sow.

Bye-bye, says the fly.